I0407392

Teaching Your Teen Behind the Wheel

A parents' guide for their teenage drivers

Written by Terry Lynn Moore

authorHOUSE

1663 LIBERTY DRIVE, SUITE 200
BLOOMINGTON, INDIANA 47403
(800) 839-8640
www.authorhouse.com

First published by AuthorHouse 08/19/04

ISBN: 1-4184-9451-8 (sc)

Printed in the United States of America
Bloomington, Indiana

This book is printed on acid-free paper.

Table of Contents

Introduction

As parents, we put a lot of work into our children when it comes to college and their futures, but it seems we too often leave out common things that are important for the safety and welfare of our children. The subject that I'm referring to is driving an automobile.

Did you know the number one cause that takes our children's lives is the automobile? That's right; from the ages of fifteen to twenty-four the main cause of death in the United States is automobile accidents.

There has been a lot of concern in relation to this subject from many parents who have children that will soon be driving on the road and parents who have a child that has been in a bad wreck or even killed. Some of our states have added extra restrictions to newly driving teenagers (i.e. the graduated license laws), hoping they will create a safer driving environment for them, but many states have done nothing.

We need to face the fact that our children are starting to drive at a very young age, which is a very pressuring and confusing time in their lives.

I am a driver education instructor, and I have had thousands of hours of experience instructing students, both behind the wheel and in the classroom. I have chosen to write this book to honor God by giving a helping hand to parents through sharing the things I have observed and learned over the years. Hopefully, it will motivate and educate parents with some effective means of teaching and interacting with their sons or daughters.

I believe the habits a new driver starts with are the same habits that will stick with him for years to come, but sadly, the teenager's bad driving habits often outweigh his good habits. The keys here are the parents.

Parents teach their children to eat, tie their shoes, help them with their schoolwork, and so many other things that induce their child to form or create a habit. Parents have an incredible influence on their children, even if the parent is not aware of it.

Over all the years I have spent in the car with students, probably the number one subjects a child talks about are his parents.

If you want to take a greater interest in the safety of your children when the years of driving come, or if you just want to be a better driver yourself, then I believe this book will be beneficial to you. This book is a tool of motivation and illustration and a manual for preparing you and your children.

Some of the topics and subjects I have included in this book are:

- Are you scared to ride with your teenager?

- Do you lack patience with your teenage driver?

- Would you like to know some of the best methods to prevent accidents?

- Would you like to see your son or daughter have faster results in their driving performance, which will result in greater safety on the road?

Of course, reading this book cannot guarantee the safety of you or your child. Like anything you do, the amount you apply is the measuring device for results you get.

This will be an enjoyable book for anyone who has children, and it will benefit their family.

Acknowledgement

First and foremost, I want to thank God for all the many years of safe driving for my students and myself He has given us. He has given me the desire to share the knowledge and experience I have received to help motivate parents and teenagers to be safer on the road.

I would like to thank my loving wife who has supported me through all the high-stress times which come with this type of job.

<u>Starting with the Right Perspective</u>

Through the years, many people have told me that they cannot comprehend how I can tolerate being in a car with inexperienced teenage drivers. They have made comments like, "I bet you have to take a pill for your nerves before you get out on the road with those kids."

It may seem like the job of a driver education instructor is the worst possible career anyone could ever imagine. If I were to give you an overview of my line of work, I would tell you that it can be strenuous and daunting at times, and those times are coming more frequently than they used to.

When I first started in this line of work, I was concerned about the risks involved, but as time went on. I learned to cope with the dangers that came with this job.

It did not take me long to realize that I needed a technique to get the results I wanted out of my students. One of the first things I learned was the importance behind the way you talk to a student in a car. You must take into consideration that almost all teenagers are incredibly nervous when they begin driving. If you yell, shout, or raise your voice at them in the wrong way, you could lose their trust, patience, and willingness to listen. They will clam up their emotions, which will greatly affect their coordination and your ability to instruct them.

I highly recommend that when you begin teaching your teenager behind the wheel, you should always try to pick a day when you will feel the most relaxed. Never go out to instruct your teenager when you are having a bad day. Remember, your emotions or those of your driver will impact and influence the quantity and quality of the teaching and learning that takes place.

Whenever you get into a car with your teenagers, never hand them the keys and say, "Well, let's see how you are going to do today," and tell them to take off. You want to get their minds in gear and thinking about the important things they are about to learn. They will be using the senses of their bodies to drive, so they need to be prepared just like they are going to engage in any sport activity. This does not mean they should actually begin doing physical exercises before they get into a car, but it means adjusting their minds, hands, feet, and eyes so they will be ready for the driving task.

The procedure for getting ready to drive is called "pre-ignition" and "starting the car." When you and your child get into a car, you want to go over a few procedures to get him in his "get ready" mode. At this point, it is important to have your child's attention and to create an atmosphere that will encourage him to think.

The first thing you want to tell him to do is to lock the doors. Tell them it is the driver's duty to make sure that every one in the car has their door locked. It's much safer for the doors to be locked, because in a wreck, the car will buckle, bend, twist, and the door could come open or get knocked off. You could even get a foot or hand caught within the door in a crash. Some people have a fear of getting trapped in their vehicle from locking their doors, but it is more likely that an unlocked door will become jammed, trapping the driver, than it is for a locked door to do so. Locked doors help to sturdy the frame of a car in a wreck. Also, locking the doors helps to protect the driver and passengers from anyone trying to jump into the car unexpectedly, such as the case with car-jacking crimes.

The second part of pre-ignition and starting the car is to adjust the seat so the driver's leg and foot reaches comfortably to the pedals. Tell your driver to apply the gas and then the brake with only his right foot to see if the seat feels comfortable as he shifts between the two. Then, ask him to adjust the back of his seat so that he can comfortably put his wrist on top of the steering wheel while his back is firm or flat against the seat.

The driver being at ease and relaxed while driving will help him to have better control over the car and will help prevent him from being worn out so quickly while driving.

I have found that many students are not able to drive their best, simply because they are not comfortable and do not have their seats adjusted properly.

Because your children are using the physical parts of their bodies to drive, they are forming instincts and habits they will keep for the rest of their lives. When you are instructing your son or daughter, do not think of this as a temporary moment of instruction that you can rush through. Remember, the more that is said about each procedure, the more your teenager will pick up, understand, and learn.

My feelings on this is to over-teach, because as we all know, a lot of what we teach our children will go in one ear and right out the other, and they rarely will tell you when they did not understand something. Test your teenager each and every time he goes out for driving practice to see what he is learning. Never assume he understands anything you have only said once or twice or three times.

You want to go over a few more parts of pre-ignition and starting the car, such as adjusting the steering wheel, the head rest, and restraints each time you drive with him to show him that he should do this every time he gets in the car. Make sure you take plenty of time talking about the mirrors on the car. Ask him what he is seeing out of the mirrors and what he cannot see. Tell your teenager to sit just like he is driving down the road with both hands on the wheel and to glance at the mirrors to test if they are adjusted correctly.

Another part of the pre-ignition and starting the car method is putting your seatbelt on and making sure that every one in the car has theirs on as well. Here again, you want to give a lot of explanation for this procedure through providing good examples, so the student will understand the purpose behind what you are trying to teach him. For example, if you are only traveling twenty miles per hour and another car hits you head-on at only twenty miles per hour, then that is some what like ramming your car into a brick wall at forty miles per hour. You are not trying to scare your driver, but you want to educate and plant all kinds of warning signals in your son's or daughter's mind, so that he or she will have this to remind him or her when he or she is on his or her own.

There are many days that I see former students driving without their seatbelts on. Sometimes, people think nothing bad can ever happen to them. Out of the forty to fifty thousand people that die every year in vehicle accidents, you can be sure of one thing—a large majority of them died because of not wearing their seatbelts.

Before your new driver heads out on the road, you need to stress some very important safety facts. First, you want to talk to him about taking selective glances as he drives. This is called the I.P.D.E. process, which means: identify, predict, decide, and execute. This process trains the driver to use his eyes more effectively, efficiently, and to have a greater awareness of what is going on around him as he drives. The more a driver moves his eyes, the more he will see. This does not happen instinctively. This method is the foundation of what allows a driver to receive the right information which allows him to respond accordingly.

Identify means to use the most important sense of the body as you drive—your vision. You want to teach your teenager to form a habit of never starring or letting his eyes fixate in one place too long while he is behind the wheel. He should practice under your supervision the technique of glancing to the sides of the car, glancing straight ahead, glancing in the mirrors, glancing at the speedometer, and scanning all intersections and driveways.

It is your duty as a parent to work hard with your teenager on the scanning process. You will know, as you drive with him, if he is seeing every thing as one big picture. You can test your teenager every time you go out by asking him questions such as: what color was that car that just went by, or did you see that on coming car hugging the yellow line.

The second and third part of the I.P.D.E. process is predicting and deciding, which go hand in hand. For example, if your son or daughter is driving and he or she is approaching an intersection which cars are trying to pass through, he or she should put their foot over the brake to cut down the reaction time in case he or she has to stop suddenly. Once he are clear from danger, then he can put his foot back on the gas pedal. Teaching this technique alone could save your teenager's life. Most teenagers do not even give a crowded intersection a second thought. They drive through, maintaining a high speed with their feet on the gas. Covering the brake is much safer.

If you feel the situation ahead looks unsafe, then you can do something to prevent the accident and not add to the problem, regardless of who has the right away. Covering the brake may not sound like much, but it will knock off about three-fourths of a second to your reaction time. As fast as wrecks occur, having your foot already over the brake could easily reduce the amount of damage in a wreck, or it may even prevent a wreck from happening.

Consider this, if you do not teach your teenager about defensive driving, he will not drive defensively, and he will never expect the unexpected.

As your teenager drives, he will execute all kinds of maneuvers with his car, but it is critical that he responds correctly after he has identified, predicted, and decided, or else he will be guessing and hoping he is doing the right thing. Never forget that good driving methods and techniques have to be formed as a habit so they are stored in his brain to draw from when needed.

If the brain is void of the message that needs to be sent to the other parts of the body, then the driver is in real trouble. Children forget much of what they learn in their driver education classes, so the parents need to continue the process. Parents are concerned about their children failing tests at school, so they make them study with much repetition. The same should be so, and even more so, with the safe procedures for driving that can save their lives.

In the United States military, our children are sent to boot camp to prepare for the possibility of war, but we as parents do not put enough time into the training of our children for something that kills our children more than wars, disease, and anything else in the United States.

Teenagers are going away from their homes in automobile accidents, because they are not prepared like they should be. Extra training with your teenager is incredibly important! It is imperative that your children receive all the attention you can possibly give them, because habits form the easiest in the early years of their lives.

There is a tremendous amount of confusion and pressure on a teenager during their beginning driving years. If we want a good future for our children, we need to provide not only spiritual, academic, and financial instruction, but also instruction on safety.

The Senses of Touch and Sight

When you think of the most important part of your body you use while driving, you would probably think of the brain first, but the brain actually registers only what the eyes see when it comes to driving. As we drive, we take in so much information through our eyes. Your eyes are like cameras constantly taking pictures as you drive. If we are not careful, we will miss many hidden objects in the pictures our eyes take.

The second most important sense of the body we use to drive is the sense of touch. You need to realize from the beginning of driving, and what all new drivers need to never forget, is that the sense of feel is sharper than eye sight.

Think about when a mosquito bites you, sometimes you will feel the bite and never see the insect. You should never trust your eyes to do all of the work. It is impossible to even drive a vehicle without the right sense of touch.

The new driver has to learn how to feel what the car is trying to do as it goes down the road. The sensitivity of the car's devices, like power steering and brakes, can make it tough on the new driver sometimes. Each new driver needs to be taught that the faster a car is moving, then the more sensitive the steering will be and less movement is needed. Let them know as they steer straight forward to use tiny movements on the wheel, what I refer to as micro-movements.

Make sure from day one you tell them about the dangers of jerking the steering wheel. Instruct your student to make adjustments and readjustments on the wheel all along. Explain to your teenager that if he moves the wheel in one direction, then he will have to move it back. This probably sounds like pretty basic, but it is stuff teenagers often do not think about and they really need to know.

Most parents will think these basic concepts are not necessary and their teenagers will figure this out on their own. From what I have learned over the years, if you leave these basic techniques out and do not work with your children diligently with these effective methods, then your teenager will be much less prepared to drive than what he could have been, and it is often these things that cause accidents.

It is easy for a new driver to over-steer or under-steer when they first start. A new driver will be nervous, even if they say they are not. His nerves will cause him to clam up a little and sometimes a lot. This will force the driver to over-steer or to under-steer.

As you teach your teenager, you need to be aware of how your son or daughter is feeling as he or she drives. Ask them now and then to relax and take a light grip on the wheel. Tell your driver to relax his back, shoulders, arms, and hands.

I have noticed when I say this to my drivers, I can immediately see a result in the way they begin steering.

When you notice he is griping the wheel tightly and tensing up, just get him to relax again. This will become a habit for him soon, and his steering will get better.

As your student drives down a road, ask him which way the car is pulling. This will also make him concentrate when he knows he has to give you an answer.

I have instructed my students while they were driving to take their hands off the wheel completely while I used my left hand to steer the car. I would even remove my left hand a few inches away from the wheel so the driver could tell me which way the car was moving. I would grab the wheel before the car went too far to the left or the right.

By learning to judge the sensitivity of the wheel the driver can see the importance of how the eyes respond slower than "feeling the wheel". The student would realize that he could not rely on just the eyes to keep their car in his lane.

I hope you can see by some of these examples that you should approach your teenager at different angles when teaching him how to drive.

One of the contributing factors in teenager-related wrecks is that the driver jerks the wheel on the vehicle when he runs off the road or sometimes when he thinks he is going to run off. New drivers have a huge fear of running off the road. Your new driver needs to know the concepts of what happens when you run off the road. It is not dangerous to run off, but it can be dangerous if you get back on incorrectly.

When I have a driver that wants to jerk the wheel and gets, what I refer to as, "real jumpy," then I pull him off the road at a low speed, when no one is behind us, to get that fear out of him and to show them there is nothing of which to be afraid. My hand is very close to the wheel to make sure the driver does not jerk the wheel or pull back on it too hard. This is called "off road recovery."

If parents would carefully work with their children about off road recovery, then I believe the death toll of teenagers running off the road and jerking their wheels would come down dramatically. Because of damaged roads, the tires grabbing the raised edge of the road, and loss of traction, teenagers need to be more prepared for occasionally running off the road, so they will know how to handle it when it happens.

The sense of touch is also very important when using the gas and brake pedals. If your son or daughter starts driving by making you kiss the windshield and giving you whiplash, then he or she most likely does not have his or her foot adjusted properly. Make sure he uses his ankle and the ball of his foot to do all the pressing and not his heel or the whole leg. Take your hand and press on their arm the amount of pressure they should apply. You will have put up with a lot of unsmooth actions from him for a while, but it will come with practice. It will be very helpful if you say all along to your driver, "When you stop and start, be smooth with the pedals." This is something I have said many times during my driving session when I have a lead- or heavy-footed driver.

As you practice with your teenager, it is important that you make sure he is using his eyes properly. Your eyes go hand in hand with the sense of touch, so the driver needs to always keep his eyes moving. A new driver will have a tendency to stare or to look too long at one thing.

Usually, the driver will pull toward at what he is staring. To drive safely, the driver needs to make eye contact with many different objects as he goes down the road to keep him alert of his surroundings.

New drivers are not used to moving their eyes when they first start to drive, and they only want to watch the road or the car in front of them. They have to be trained to pick up on all kind of clues of what pertains to the driving scene. As our children are growing up, they pick up bad habits of staring at the television set or the computer screen. While driving, the student has to fight against those old habits and create some new ones.

Using your eyes to know what is around you at all times is always important. The key instruments to help with this are your mirrors, when used properly. Let him know that the further away an object gets from the car, the amount he can view in his mirrors increases. The closer an object gets to the car, the amount he can view in his mirrors decreases. This is one of the ways you are teaching your teenager to use his eyes properly.

You also want to instruct your teenager to look over his shoulders to get a better view of his rear and side, especially when changing lanes and backing up. Let them know of how new drivers get into many wrecks, because they did not use their mirrors properly and check their blind spots.

While you practice with your teenager, put him to a test each and every time you take him out on the road. Pick out something that is wrong on the road, such as a pothole, and ask your driver if he saw it. It could be that the oncoming car was hugging or crossing the center line, or some one ahead did not fully stop at an intersection. The more you hold him accountable to what he is seeing, the more he will see and the safer he will drive because you are helping him create safer driving habits.

It takes time and patience working with your children, so keep on telling them about the importance of their steering, keeping their eyes moving, taking selective glances, seeing everything as one big picture, and to be easy and smooth with the steering wheel and pedals. The more you imbed this in their minds, the more they will remember.

Terry Lynn Moore

The Right Attitude

With anything you do in life, when you have a good attitude, you receive and accomplish much more out of what you are trying to achieve. Much of the time, a teenage driver may drive a car well, when it comes to driving skills, but his attitude controls the outcome of what he is doing.

From all my experience in the classroom and behind the wheel, I have seen how most students are really lacking when it comes to good social skills. If they hear a lot of complaining, yelling, or arguing from their parents, then you can expect them to be the same way. Parents are constantly painting a picture for their children of how to view and relate to the world. The time God has given us to be real parents is a very short time, and we have to use it wisely. Some of us have wasted a large portion of the time we have with our children, and then we wonder why we have the relationship with our children that we do.

It's true that the teenage years can be a tough time, but if we would live the life we are trying to teach our children and set a good example, then they would not just hear our instructions, they would also see them.

If a child constantly does not pay attention in a classroom, dislikes his teachers, or has problems getting along with others while he is growing up, then this will be a habit he has worked hard to form over a long period of time. When he gets old enough to drive, he will take the same attitude or habits to the automobile. It is not like when his driving days begin, he will automatically drop all of his bad habits and keep only his good ones.

Our children spend a massive amount of time behind the screens of TVs, computers, and video games. If all these were used moderately and what they portrayed was right for our children, then these things could be a benefit. But let's face it; most households are full of long hours of TV and computer games, and a lot of these programs are teaching our children impatience and that it is "okay" to be angry when you do not get your way.

Children need to learn how to interact with others at a young age. I have noticed that teenagers more and more do not like to be told what to do and dislike receiving instructions. When I am teaching my students behind the wheel, sometimes I feel like I am on pins and needles. I have to use particular words so the student will not feel like I am scolding him, but I know I am only trying to instruct them. I think so much of this comes from them seeing adults setting bad examples—getting frustrated or angry when some body pulls out in front of us, showing impatience toward our neighbor, and getting angry over minor things.

If our children are raised in an environment where there is no respect for authority, then they will probably be the same way. Please, do not take this the wrong way and think that I am referring to all families. I know there are really good parents that care and go through a lot to ensure their children are brought up right, but I am seeing this less and less. Even if you are guilty of some of the things I have mentioned, it does not mean that you are a bad parent; it just means we all can improve in some of these areas.

When we think of a severe form of having a bad attitude on the road, we would most likely think of "road rage." People are killed in accidents all the time because of this strong attitude problem. Showing love and forgiveness towards others is a sign of control. When our children see this in us, they see strength, stability, and comfort. If we are teaching them compassion while they grow up, this will nourish their mental health. Think about this, if you are inconsiderate of others on the road all the time and could care less how others feel around you when you interact with them on the road, then you would pass illegally, tailgate, run stop signs, do roll stops, pull out in front of others, speed, and no telling what else. Would you want your son or daughter to practice these habits? Try to do every thing you can to prevent your children from developing "road rage" habits. You do not have to drive down the road with a gun in your hand to begin the "road rage" attitude.

When you are instructing your son or daughter behind the wheel, try to communicate as clearly as possible. Let him or her know when you repeat yourself that you are not mad, but just keeping everyone safe. If he never reacts to your instruction, go over the reasons why he did not instead of yelling at him. Talk to your teenagers about all the problems they will face on the road and tell them to not take your instruction so personally. Teach them to learn from other people's mistakes instead of condemning them; they could make some of the same mistakes.

Also, teach your teenager to never drive when they are upset or mad. Let them know how easy this can impair their ability to think clearly and drive safely. Get your teenagers to give you a report on what went on as they drove for that day when they are on their own with their licenses. Make them think back on all the instructions you have given them. Believe me, they will remember what you have taught them when they do something wrong in their vehicle, if you have taught them in love.

Your actions speak so loudly that sometimes your children cannot hear a word you are saying. Show love and understanding, try not to grudgingly teach, and they will receive a great gift that will help them for a lifetime. Remember, that courtesy is contagious, and we should treat others on the road the way we want to be treated.

Judging Space and Distance

If you were to ask most teenagers if they had good control over their automobiles, they probably would not even hesitate to answer you, "Of course I do." Having good control of the automobile as you drive means a wide range of things. It does not require a lot of skill to drive your car down a road or even to stop your car, but it is a different story to have good car control.

There are many different kinds of maneuvers that can be performed to greatly enhance your driving ability. One thing that makes a teenager so dangerous on the road is the lack of basic car control. Teaching your son or daughter to judge his or her space and distance is a very important part of basic car control and can very well mean the difference between a safe driver and an unsafe driver.

You may be thinking, "How is this relevant to basic car control?"

When most teenagers and other drivers get in an accident, they do not crash suddenly and for no reason. Most of the time, if you investigate a crash scene, you will see that space and distance was a major factor for the wreck. Let me go over some drills you can teach and should use on a regular basis to help new drivers.

First, let us look at the following distance you should have from another vehicle. While you are instructing your son or daughter behind the wheel, tell him or her to pick a fixed point on the side of the road, like a parked car, tree, building, or a sign. When the car in front of him gets to that fixed point, then he needs to count off seconds, like one thousand and one, one thousand and two, and so on. The average following distance they should be from that car is two seconds. This works well at any speed as long as the conditions are ideal (no rain, sleet, snow, construction, heavy traffic, etc.).

If the conditions are not ideal, then you would increase your following distance and decrease your speed. You need to maintain this distance in order to have good basic car control. The reason for this is your car cannot stop in time, no matter how mechanically superior your car is or how good your traction is. If the car in front of you suddenly stops, you could hit them.

If you hit someone in the rear, then you will be considered at fault, and you will be one of the many people that contribute to high insurance premiums. Not only do these types of collisions add to high insurance rates, but they are very popular among teenagers. There is no excuse for this type of wreck. It shows the driver in fault was tailgating (following too closely) and was not being thoughtful of the other driver. You could easily injure someone's spine, and they could have problems with this the rest of their life. There is always a chance that you could make the other car run off the road or have a head-on collision with someone in the other lane. It is important to stress to your teenagers that tailgating is illegal, rude, and dangerous! Always teach them that patience is very rewarding and impatience causes drivers to take dangerous and stupid risks.

As I am talking about space and distance, let us look at the area on the road where most accidents occur. That is where drivers' paths cross each other the most— intersections. Old habits of touch and go stops, roll stops (never coming to a complete stop), and looking straight forward at a green light have killed many people over the years. If you drive like this in front of your son or daughter, then you are showing him or her how to live very dangerously. It takes time for the brain to receive what your eyes have seen. You need to look every way when you will cross someone's path at least twice.

You also need to "count the seconds" any where you are going to enter the road, so it will help you judge the space and distance you need to get out. That way, you will know how much time you have by technique and not just guessing.

As you practice with your new driver, have him to count off seconds to see how long it takes to get out at intersections, making left turns, right turns, and going straight. Let him count off seconds while he is waiting for traffic to clear at different speed zones. This will help him judge his space and distance.

I have noticed a lot of stop signs where the stop line—the wide, white paint stripe that you are supposed to stop behind—is set back too far. The best thing to teach your children at these places is to stop close to the road, not in the road, where you can see clearly and you will reduce the time gap between your car and where the road begins. This way, they will get out much quicker when it is clear.

A good rule at traffic lights is to scan for traffic always, even if your light has been green for a while. When you are sitting at a red light and it turns green, do not tell your teenager to take off or go, but while he is taking his foot off the brake to put it onto the gas pedal, tell him to look both ways first. This will help keep him safe at intersections without intimidating anyone else at the intersection.

I hope you can see how it is not always steering or speeding, but also how a driver judges his space and distance and handles intersections. These give him the basic control skills he needs.

Any maneuver that is performed with the vehicle should be done with as much understanding as possible. It is very easy to misjudge your space and distance if your teenager practices bad habits. Without using the right techniques, he will never draw away from his bad habits.

Always practice in a place where it requires more of the driver's attention, like intersections. Never assume your teenager sees the driving scene the way you do. You have a lot more experience than he does. Think of how it was when you first started to drive; you were nervous, easily intimidated, and not so sure of what to do at times. All of these, plus car headlights, rain, unfamiliar roads, and conditions, can add to his driving difficulty. How much knowledge he has stored up will prove effective when necessary and will be the most helpful tool that will help make him a safe driver.

Terry Lynn Moore

Tight Speed Control

When first learning to drive, your top priority should be to have good basic control over the automobile you are driving. You have probably heard the saying, "You need to learn to walk before you run." People have a tendency to be so impatient when it comes to learning anything new. They skip steps and leave out the most important parts.

There are certain measures or steps a new driver needs to practice and get used to before he can have proficient control over the vehicle. A lot of parents leave things out due to their impatience and lack of knowing how to go about instructing their children.

When you apply your instructions to your teenager, you need to go over a lot of the same things in a repetition which will induce memorization. Always let your instruction and how you teach to be conducted with quality. Never

37

throw a bunch of rules and instructions at your son or daughter and expect him or her to receive it the first few times he or she hears it. Try not to get ahead of the progress he or she is making and go at his or her pace. Think of how you were instructed when you were a beginner behind the wheel, and think about what style of instruction helped you learn the best.

New drivers often do not understand the concept of driving faster than they can operate a vehicle. They think you have to press the gas pedal to make the car move and when something goes wrong, they only have to apply the brake to safely stop, but this is not true.

At the very beginning of instructing your children behind the wheel, it is important to tell them that the strongest part of their body is their legs, and it is very easy to push too hard with them.

If you will compare how we rest our forearm or wrist when we use a key board with the computer to resting their heel on the floor when applying the brake and gas pedal, it will be a great help.

The ankle should be thought of as a hinge. This way, they will be more precise with the amount of pressure they apply. You should have them to press the gas and brake several times going back and forth while the car is running but still in park. This is very important! I would not dare think of letting them take off without having a good idea of the amount of pressure they need to apply to the pedals first. This will also help them get their feet adjusted properly and comfortably, and this will tell them if their seats are in the right position.

Never allow your teenager to use both feet to drive a car. This will cause a coordination conflict. The brain will have to do one extra duty to stop the car, and in a hazardous situation, it is more likely he will end up pressing the gas and brake pedal at the same time.

People who drive like this also run the risk of damaging the brakes and transmission of their car. The driver, while using only the right foot, should slide his heel on the floor to go from the gas to the brake pedal and never lift his heel off the floor. If he picks up his heel, he will put his foot back down in different spots on the pedals, which will make it more difficult for him to judge how hard to press and cause coordination problems.

Be sure to show your new driver how the brake has a range of motion—the distance you press it—that allows you to stop at different rates. The range of motion will differ on every car that you drive, but it is still valuable to learn how to judge pedal pressure.

The main concept here is for the driver to understand is that the more he applies the brake, the more it will slow the car and that he does not have to press the brake hard every time he wants to slow down.

You also want to talk about pressing down on the brake to slow down and maintain control before you make a turn. Spend a lot of time practicing with your son or daughter going around a residential block making left and right turns. This will help him or her greatly understand what it takes to have good control of the vehicle while performing these maneuvers.

Pulling into and out of parking spaces is also another beneficial drill to do with your teenagers. They need to practice being in parking lots with their feet on the brakes as much as possible, because if they stay on the gas pedals and suddenly need to stop, this is going to take away from the small amount of time they already had by requiring them to switch pedals. Tell them that the speeds in these areas need to be a slow coasting speed. Too many "bump-ups" happen in parking lots.

Young drivers are usually overly eager and impatient, giving them too much determination to get started. They want to "go, go, go," even in tight spots. The new driver needs to realize that if he tries to perform with his vehicles in this manner, then he will lose his reaction time and crash.

How would you like for your son or daughter to come home to you one day after he or she has their license and tell you that he or she scraped the whole side of some body's car in a parking lot? Take the steps to prevent this ahead of time!

As a parent, you should desire for your children to have great driving habits with a good knowledge of tight speed control over their vehicles. This will not be something that they will most likely create for themselves. They will create habits of certain performances with their cars based on peer-pressure and youthful goofing-off, but this is where you can warn them and prepare them for what they can and cannot possibly do in a car.

When your teenager first starts to drive, he will be at a low level of skill. You need to make sure he goes into the next level of skill with the right concepts so he will leave all those bad habits behind.

It is scary to think about how some students will start off on the road with their licenses at nearly the same level as when they had their permit. That will mean students will go in reverse when you told them to go forward and then look at you and ask, "Doesn't R mean run?"

I hope you will see the need of tight speed control and will work with your teenager to help him go to the next level of keeping his vehicle safely in, out, and around tight places in which he will constantly have to drive.

The speed of the vehicle greatly affects the control that the driver really has over his driving spot.

Terry Lynn Moore

Traction on the Road

Have you heard the saying, "Your life is riding on your tires while you drive?" As you should know, God is giving you the protection you need anytime you are out on the road. But although God is a sovereign, He has given us the responsibility to take care of ourselves. There is still some truth in, "Your life is riding on your tires." When we walk up to our car, we like to view it as one big piece of machinery that hugs the road firmly and tightly. This is a very common misconception among teenagers. The truth of the matter is, your car grabs the road with four spots as big as your hand. That is not a lot of grip. Does that change how you view your car? The entire car does not grip the road, but it is holding on by four little spots.

Here is something you need to do with your student driver. While your car is parked on pavement, take a piece of chalk and make a mark as close as possible around the tire where it meets the pavement. After you move the car, you can show the marks to your teenager and explain to him that when the car is moving, the tires lift a little. So, the mark he is seeing now would be smaller, and it gets even smaller the greater your speed.

Also, take into consideration that the traction we have as we drive is interfered with by so many things—rain, leaves, sand, gravel, oil, ice, snow, worn tires, and damaged roads.

Try this demonstration. Tell your teenager to rub his hands together with about five pounds of pressure and holding his hands horizontal to the floor. Then, tell him to put a piece of paper in between his hands doing the same thing. This will give him the right idea of how anything that gets between his tires and the road will cause a loss of traction. Although this may sound somewhat childish, he will probably remember it for a long time. A picture paints a thousand words, and it sure will make your instructions a little more interesting.

When you are instructing your teenager, use creative examples that will force him to think. Try to never limit your teaching to "do this," "don't do this," or a "listen only to me" session. A child will learn much more if you make it interesting and create an atmosphere where he is not just being drilled with instructions.

Loss of traction often occurs when a new driver uses his brake too heavily or in the wrong place. Too many students regard the brakes as something that can miraculously stop a problem just by applying a little pressure when something goes wrong.

It is important that your teenager understands how the vehicle he is driving functions. My cars that I used for driver education are only equipped with a brake and not a gas pedal. When students apply their brakes in the wrong places, I have no way of undoing what they have just done. All I can do is verbally instruct them of what to do. That is why it is also important to help your driver understand what will cause him to put himself in danger.

Giving plenty of explanations on the importance of traction for stopping, slowing, and making turns will be helpful, but it is not enough. Your teenager needs to be taught when to brake, where to brake, and how much to brake. Do plenty of stops with your teenager when he first starts to drive. Take him to a place where there is practically no traffic, such as an empty parking lot, and have him to do some quick stops where he will come just short of skidding. Make sure there is no one behind you and keep your hand close to the steering wheel. After he gets the feel of what is to hard, then he will know more about the right amount of braking to keep traction.

The tires on your vehicle should always be in good shape to enhance safety and to save fuel. Sometimes, a nail or tack may lodge in your tire and let the air out slowly. Cold weather can cause the tires to deflate some as well. Tires that do not have the proper amount of air in them will wear out sooner and are not as safe on which to drive. You will save money if the tires wear out evenly, because they will last longer when the entire rubber grips the road. You also save gas when the car is rolling smooth. Of course, the point here is that the tire will grip the road better when the proper air is in it. The treads on the tires also play an important roll in wet weather. A tire with good treads will allow water to disperse away from the tire, so you have less chance of hydroplaning (sliding across water).

This is common sense knowledge you need to share with your children. Think of it like this: if your son or daughter is going to drive on a freeway with four badly worn tires, and one of them has low air pressure, adding rain to this could spell disaster! Let your teenager know how expensive tires are and that he should be responsible for them. Tires on small vehicles, which most teenagers drive, should last two to three years. When a teenager wears them out in less than a year, you can pretty much figure out what kind of stops, turns, and take-offs he is making.

Everyone who drives will eventually lose control of their vehicles. That may sound like a strong statement, but it is true. I am sure you can name a few of your own experiences. The cause could be rain, snow, ice, sand, running off the road, etc. It is one thing to lose control and crash, but of course, another to lose control and then regain control.

The method here you need to teach your teenager is to turn the wheel in the direction you are skidding. You can also tell him to point the car back in the direction he wants to go to simplify things. Let him know if he gets into a situation like this, he will most likely over-steer due to panic. The key here is to not panic and to try to slow the movement of the wheel without slamming on the brakes, which could cause the car to go even more out of control.

Every time you take your student out for driving practice, you need to go over what he should do so it will be instinctual for later use. Even if a teenager forgets a lot of these important points about traction, he may remember at least enough to save his life. Never feel that you need to leave out something. Make sure that your son or daughter gets a grip of the importance of traction on the road.

Terry Lynn Moore

Driving in High Risk Areas

There are many places on the road on which parents really need to focus when teaching their teenagers how to drive safely. Keep in mind that there are multiple places on the road that may not appear to be hazardous, but this could be a misconception. A strong point you should emphasize with your children is to always expect the unexpected. Let us first look at some of the areas people overlook as being a hazard or to which they pay too little of attention.

One area that is often overlooked would be passing. We all know that people pass frequently and nearly anywhere they can. You will even see people passing on solid yellow lines, in the middle of curves, hills, bridges, and even when there is oncoming traffic. This makes driving on a two lane road very dangerous. The most severe wreck anyone can ever be involved in occurs on two lane roads—a head-on collision.

If you are traveling fifty-five miles per hour and you hit a car head-on that is going fifty-five, then that is a 110 mile per hour impact! That is like an explosion! Think about the weight of the vehicles involved. If one weighs about four thousand pounds and the other about three thousand, imagine the force of the impact. That is seven thousand pounds of machinery colliding at 120 miles per hour. Another way to look at this is to imagine ramming your car into a brick wall at 110 miles per hour. You would be incredibly blessed if you survived.

Teaching your teenager that it is okay to pass whenever they want to, can make him an impatient driver. It is a fact; being impatient on the road means you will take more risk without even giving yourself the proper time to weigh the cost. This is something you want to avoid doing to your new driver.

From day one, you need to put a lot of emphases on just how dangerous it is to pass another vehicle on the road. You should teach children to know that when you pass, you should not just think about yourself, but you also have to consider the driver you are passing. Every time you pass someone, you are hoping and trusting while you go around them that they will not speed up or swerve. You could start going around a car and suddenly notice another car coming at you, and you may decide to not pass. If the car you are trying to pass panics or slows a lot, then you are stuck. I know this might seem negative, but it is being defensive. Children need to know that a lot of things can go wrong when passing and, in reality, what their chances are while trying to perform certain tasks.

Make sure you instruct your teenager about all the points of conflict that can be a threat to him when it comes to passing. Tell him about how hills affect his speed, how far he should see ahead if he is going to pass, and how easy it is to misjudge his space. Help your son or daughter understand the concepts of judging the necessity to pass.

Rushing often does not save as much time as most people think. If you are going to travel thirty miles and drive five miles per hour over the speed limit, you will save very few minutes. Those few minutes are not worth risking your license, higher insurance rates, and your life. If we teach this concept to our children and set an example, some of this will influence them. If you always drive in a rush, then expect your children to probably do the same thing.

While your teenager is learning to drive, have him to drive around for thirty miles. Tell him to keep it five miles per hour under the speed limit, so he can see for himself what little time he lost. When he returns, tell him to stay with the speed limit. See, now you are giving your teenager another picture in his head, instead of the dangerous habit of rushing.

Teach him to make his time up at home, not on the road. Monitor your teenager when he gets his license to see if he is trying to create habits of leaving late, instead of leaving a little early and driving safer. I believe if parents will work with their children as they grow up, to be patient and set a good example for them, it will make a big difference in the choices they make and the way they approach life.

Intersections are also very high risk areas. As a matter of fact, more accidents occur at intersections than any other place on the road. A lot of people do not realize how dangerous an intersection is. One of the things that makes it prone to bad accidents is the risk of side-on collisions which occur most often at these points in the road. Because the worst possible crash you could get into is the head-on collision, then probably the second to that would be a side-on collision.

Think about it; in a side-on collision there is very little protection from the car hitting you. The car a teenager will drive is probably going to be a small car. That means the car doors will be very thin. So, a driver needs to give himself as much protection as possible by being alert.

Perhaps you are thinking, "I do not want my son's or daughter's car to be very big, so they can handle it better. Nor do I want it to weigh very much, so it will not hit so hard if there is a wreck." The lighter the car is, the less protection the driver of that car has. Teenagers desire to drive small cars because of their appearance, not because of their safety. The passenger sits lower to the road where she or he cannot see as well. If a small car is in a wreck with a pick up truck, sport utility vehicle, or any other taller vehicle, the driver of the smaller car can be very seriously injured or killed. It does not have to be a severe type of accident for someone to get hurt severely.

The number one thing you want to teach your driver at intersections is to look very thoroughly before pulling out or going through. This is a very important point to stress to a new driver. Remember, it takes time for your mind to receive the message that your eyes have photographed. If you make a quick glance and go, then you are not giving yourself enough time to be safe. You want to tell your teenager to look both ways at least twice before pulling out anywhere. Tell him that sometimes when he drives, he will have a lot of things on his mind that will distract the message sending process. When you train him behind the wheel, make sure that you see him doing this all the time and at every place he pulls onto the road. This includes coming out of your own driveway, another danger spot on the road.

Railroad tracks are another dangerous point on the roads. Sometimes, people cross these tracks every day going to and from their homes. The point that needs to be stressed here is that a train uses those tracks as well. People depend on the mechanical devices to warn them too much. Face it; the guard rails and the red lights do not always work. Anything that is mechanical can fail at one time or another. However, that does not mean it is the railroad company's fault.

Here is some good advice on how to handle these dangerous spots. First, the trains will sound their whistles at all intersections, so you need to be able to hear this by not having your car stereo too loud. Then, you do not want to go too fast over the tracks, because they are bumpy. However, you should always have enough speed so that if your car dies on the tracks, you could keep rolling off of them. Lastly, you want to keep looking until you know it is safe. Many people are killed on railroad tracks every year in the U.S., which means it is important to practice these safety procedures a lot with your teenagers.

Another high risk area is the parking lot. I know most new drivers think that this is off the road, and it should be safe, but it is not. Many accidents happen in parking lots. Most states consider parking lots as a part of the road, and the laws are usually the same there as on a street. Some people may also think these areas are not dangerous, because the speeds are so much lower. You might want to consider this. People get struck by cars in parking lots, many teenagers have their first wrecks in parking lots, and many insurance claims are paid out every year due to parking lot accidents.

Also, keep in mind that with the small cars many teenagers like to drive, the speed of the crash does not have to be very fast for a lot of damage to be done. Many neck, feet, and back injuries that have bothered people for years, came from parking lot wrecks.

Teach your teenager to check his blind spots thoroughly in these areas and especially so while backing up. Tell him to keep his speed very low. Make sure he practices a safe speed that will give him time to prevent a wreck if someone pulls out in front of him Even if someone pulls out in his path, he could be at fault also if he is not driving the ideal speed for the conditions in which he is driving.

Also, keep in mind that it is not just the areas in which we, or our teenager, drive that make a situation high risk, but the high risk situations can also be created by the car itself. Try to encourage your new driver to take a lot of glances when he operates the devices on the car, such as the wind shield wipers, bright and dim switch for the head lights, and the stereo in the car. Tell him to always slow a little at night, because his visibility is reduced. Also, the number of passengers in the car makes a big difference.

Please, remember that just telling your teenager these things often is not enough. You need to have rules and a watchful eye in the beginning of his driving career that will force him to keep a good, clean habit.

The Impaired Driver

Most parents would be very concerned about their sons or daughters drinking and driving or being impaired by some other drug while they are trying to operate huge pieces of machinery such as automobiles. Teenagers have a fear of being left out or alone. That is when the peer pressure becomes dangerous. We live in a society where not only are we labeled by what we have or own, but also by whom our friends are and whom we know. We live in a world where children watch more TV and play more video games than nearly anything else. Think of all the programs they watch and the commercials your teenagers know, and all catchy little phrases they have learned, even from very young ages.

It is no wonder that our children do not know how to socialize with one another and pick the right friends. They think they have to have all name brand clothes, shoes, and cars. They are living lives to impress someone else.

The number one reason why a teenager does many of the "stupid" things he does is to put on a show for his friends.

When driving a vehicle, the driver needs to be in his or her best possible condition. This is even truer for teenagers, because their skills are not as sharp as someone who has been driving for years.

The best drug prevention starts at home. Parents need to teach their children at very young ages to respect themselves and how to take good care of their bodies. God has given us these wonderful bodies, and we need to teach our children the responsibility of carrying for them at young ages and as they go through their lives.

The more educated our teenagers are about the effects of drugs and alcohol, the less likely they will be influenced into trying them. They need to hear this from the ones they trust and love. If we do not give our children much love, attention, and reasons not to abuse their bodies, then they will not have a reason not to do so.

Remember, peer pressure is a strong influence on them and we need to detour them from this by giving and showing many more things that look positive to them. The mind of a teenager is very delicate and can be influenced quite easily, but if his mind is full of love from family and given strong reasons of why he should do the right thing, then there is a much better chance that he will think twice before doing something wrong and harmful.

Tell your teenagers it is not only alcohol that impairs the driver but marijuana and other drugs. There are so many teenagers using marijuana today that you would probably be shocked. Part of teaching driver education is to teach about drinking and driving and the use of other drugs. Over the years, as we have discussions in the classroom, I have noticed the degree of conversations like, "My friend does this," or "Last night I did this certain drug."

I can see that children are hungry for attention and for answers in the lives they are living. Many times, while a student was taking the "behind the wheel" part of driver education, he opened up to me about the drugs he had taken and used. I have had many students admit that all their friends had at least tried marijuana.

I am going to leave you with some facts you need to know, and I recommend any positive material that would help you show and teach your children.

The first thing that I have learned, from some of the discussions in the classroom, is that children are getting a lot of false material off the internet. I have checked out much of it. It is horrible and inaccurate! The bad thing is that most children believe it. I know this, because there is much debate in my classroom about what is true and what is not.

Remember that:

1. Alcohol plays an important part in nearly forty percent of traffic deaths.

2. Nearly half of the people that die in these wrecks have not even been drinking; the impaired driver killed the other person.

3. Just one beer or one puff of marijuana will greatly take away what is needed to drive safely.

4. Drugs will change a teenager's personality, attitude, emotions, and actions. Watch for these signs in your children. Do not assume that it is just them growing up.

5. The number one cause of death for teenagers is car accidents!

Terry Lynn Moore

Signs, Signals, and Paint

on the Pavement

Did you know a large portion of drivers view so many signs each time they drive, but do not know the full meaning of them? You could probably do a survey with one hundred people, asking questions like:

- What does a stop sign tell you to do besides stop?
- Why would a yield sign be thought of as one of the strongest signs on the road?
- What are the three basic speed rules?
- Which school sign is placed the furthest from the school?
- What vehicles have to stop at railroad crossings?
- What do the no passing zone signs have in common with the paint on the road?

- What is the difference between signs that tell you about laws you must obey and signs that tell you about surprise situations?

This survey would most likely reveal that drivers really have limited knowledge about traffic signs. If the people driving have a limited knowledge of these signs, then what about our new drivers? Just like everything you learn about driving has to be built as a habit, so does learning the meaning of signs, signals, and what the paint on the pavement means.

I am going to list a variety of signs, road markings, signals, and explain the "right away" rules in this chapter to better equip you with the right information to teach your new driver and that will most likely benefit even experienced drivers

Stop Sign: The stop sign tells you to always come to a complete stop. Remember, if you do not come to a complete stop, you will not give your brain time to receive what your eyes have seen. Stop close to the road and avoid stopping and going to ease your way closer to the stop sign, stopping only once.

This will do a few things for you. It helps prevent a rear-end collision due to pulling up more than once, and it means you will enter the road much quicker.

Remember the right away laws at stop signs. When you are making a right, yield to all traffic from your left. When you are going straight, yield to the left and right. When you are making a left, yield to every one (left, right, and straight in front of you).

In a four way stop, the car that gets there first goes first. When you are one of the three cars that arrive at the same time, then the car on the right goes first. Remember, that if four cars arrive at the same time, then some one will have to wave for one to go first

Yield Sign: To yield means letting others go before you go. Most of the time, you will find the yield sign where roads cross or merge. The yield sign is considered to be one of the strongest signs, because it can change the situation at a stop sign or traffic light. When there is a stop sign at an intersection with a yield sign on the road that merges to the right, you only have to stop if something is coming from your left.

When you are at a green or red light and making a right turn, you can also go without stopping if you have yielded completely when there is a yield sign present. Remember to treat the yield sign like a stop sign when traffic is coming. To fully yield means not pulling out in front of anyone to make them slow or stop.

One key point to remember when driving anywhere is to keep the flow of traffic moving smoothly. The driver should always think further ahead than what is going on right around your vehicle. What you do in one spot can greatly affect the close by area. We should keep in mind that our actions affect the lives of people around us.

Speed Limit Signs: The purpose of this sign is to help drivers move down the road at a safe speed. This is probably one of the most abused signs, besides the stop sign. There are three basic speed rules that go with this regulatory sign:

1. Thirty-five miles per hour in town, unless otherwise posted.
2. Fifty-five miles per hour out of town, unless otherwise posted.
3. Always drive for what the ideal conditions are.

The first and second point you need to know, because they are treated like the posted speeds, or the over all speeds, if you do not see signs. Of course, you have to adjust if the conditions are not ideal.

Here is a list of what can change the driving conditions: rain, snow, sleet, ice, fog, road construction, curvy and narrow roads, parked cars, cross walks, pedestrians, dirt and gravel roads, heavy traffic, sun glare, night driving, and the wind.

When the driving conditions change, you must adjust your driving speed accordingly. It is possible to receive a ticket for going fifty-five in a fifty-fifty miles per hour zone. The reason for this is that you are no longer driving a safe speed in heavy rain, snow, or around road construction. You may need to drop your speed to thirty-five miles per hour in rough conditions. The point here is to make sure your teenager knows the dangers out there, and makes adjustments when needed.

You need to stress to your teen driver how the speed of the car greatly affects the control he has when something goes wrong on the road. Letting your children know how they should honor and respect the laws we have should be an important part of their driving lessons. Give real life stories from the newspaper in your community for your teens to read. Teenagers do not like to watch the news, so if you do not constantly inform them on what the real dangers are, they will feel more invincible.

Warning Signs: A warning sign lets you know how to handle the road ahead. You may also say that it helps you avoid surprise situations which you can not yet see. One good way to view the warning sign is to think of it as telling you to slow down and drive with care. Here are a few examples:

Side Road Sign: This sign serves two purposes, letting you know where the location of the road ahead is, and warning you that traffic could be coming out at the road ahead. When turning onto a side road, remember they may differ, so slow down and be ready for it to be angled, narrow, or on a hill. Gravity will also react against your car on many side road turns.

School Sign: This warning sign helps protect pedestrians. The school sign has two different designs—school zone and school crossing. The one with only the pedestrians is the school zone, and the one with the cross walk is the school crossing. The school zone is placed before you get to the school. The school crossing is placed right at the school. Because of the danger of hitting a pedestrian, you could get a ticket for going a few miles per hour over the speed limit. Most residential school zones have a speed reduction of twenty five miles per hour.

The Railroad Crossing Sign: This round, yellow sign is placed before the railroad tracks. It tells you to take a few safety precautions. One would be to slow down and look both ways as you approach the track. Another would be to make sure you do not have your radio too loud, so if the train is coming, you will hear its whistle.

You should always teach your teenager, to treat every railroad crossing as if a train could be coming. The regular passenger vehicle has to be aware of a train coming, but in most states, it does not have to stop at the railroad tracks when it is clear.

All vehicles carrying sixteen or more passengers or hazardous material or waste have to stop before the tracks, even if a train is not coming.

Traffic Lights: Different lights communicate a variety of meanings to the driver. This list will help you teach the new driver a few safety precautions.

The Green Light: Always teach your student driver that green does not mean "go." It means to proceed with caution. As you know, there are no brick walls that come up to protect you when your light turns green. When the light is fresh green (just turned green), your driver should look both ways while taking his foot off the brake. This will prevent the driver from getting hit by someone that is speeding, trying to beat the red light. It will also keep the driver from holding up traffic that is behind him.

Remember, the only time you have to yield at a green light is when you make a left turn. When there is a protected left turn green arrow, the driver temporarily has the right away.

To give a clear understanding of whom you must yield to at the green light, remember you have the right away when you make a right or go straight and only have to yield to the traffic which is coming in front of you.

The Yellow Light: The solid yellow light is a warning that the traffic light is going to turn red. This may sound like common sense, but most people treat this light completely wrong. Your teenager should be taught from the very beginning how to approach a traffic light correctly. Teach your driver to never speed up at the solid yellow, but not to slam on the brakes at the last minute either. There is a point, as you get very close to the traffic light, that you must keep going. Practice with your teen, so he will have a lot of experience dealing with traffic lights before he goes out on his own.

The Red Light: Red at the traffic light means to stop. If it is legal in your state to make a right on red, remember to stop completely. Make sure there is not a sign present saying "no right on red," and fully yield the right away to any approaching traffic.

Flashing Traffic Lights: The two flashing traffic lights to which I am referring are the flashing red and the flashing yellow or caution light. The flashing red light is usually coupled with a stop sign to better get your attention. Do not forget this means stop.

The flashing yellow light (caution light) tells you to slow down and prepare to stop if necessary. This yellow light is placed at dangerous intersections.

The Paint on the Pavement: The road markings are just as important as your traffic signs and signals. They can help direct where your car needs to go or give you warnings.

The Solid Yellow Line: This marking tells you not to pass when it is on your side of the road. The double solid yellow line means both sides of traffic can not pass. This means the same as a no passing zone sign.

The Broken Yellow Line: This means you may pass with care and you are on a two lane road. Passing is considered to be one of the most dangerous maneuvers on a two lane road. Please, stress this to your new driver.

The Broken White Line: This marking separates lanes of traffic going in the same direction. Most of the time, this would mean multilane roads.

The Solid White Line: The white line guides your car in your lane. Usually, the driver should not cross the white line. These lines get worn down on two lane roads, which can make it harder to stay in your lane at night, especially when it is raining.

Arrows on the Road: The arrows tell the driver which way he may go for the lane in which he is. They also give you direction on where to turn.

Your new driver should be taught to be aware of traffic blocking these arrows on the road with his vehicle. This can get you caught in the wrong lane sometimes. Look for assisting signs with arrows on them at some intersections to help. Make sure you go over all pavement markings with your teen or new driver. All of these markings will make it safer for the new driver, if they follow what each one teaches.

I would highly recommend that you go over all the signs, signals, and paint on the pavement with your teen till you can ask about anyone of them and he could tell you without hesitation. A new driver will have no idea what to do out on the road, if he does not have a lot of information in his head already.

Getting the Permit and

the Driving Scene

So, your son or daughter has gotten to the age to begin driving. This could be an experience that not only is uncomfortable for the parent, but also for the student. If you live in a state that offers driver education, then this will be very helpful. You need to keep in mind that, just like any other teacher, the instructor could be a very good one or a very bad one. When your child takes this class, you need to get involved as a parent. I do not mean you have to embarrass your son or daughter by sitting in his or her driver education classroom, but every day they take the class, you should ask them, "What did they learn today?" Plus, see if they are taking notes.

A lot of parents have very little knowledge about what is taught in the classroom part of driver education. Some may think it is just bloody car crash movies and talking about driving.

Well, it should consist of topics such as the driver's attitude, thinking, seeing, processes, using his senses, knowing what it is to have basic control of the vehicle, the capabilities that the vehicle has, driving in adverse conditions, driving in town and cities, driving in rural areas, intersections, signs, road markings, gravity, traction, force of impact, seatbelts, handling emergencies, and teachings on drinking and driving and other drugs. This is just some of the main things, but not all of them.

Driver education is just a basic foundation safety course. I do think it is very necessary and really makes a difference in a new driver's performance, but this should be considered to be just the beginning. The learner's permit should be seen as the parents time to be the instructor.

In the state where I instruct, teenagers are required to keep their permit for a full year. Sadly, but true, a lot of parents will practice with their teenagers for a little while, but not nearly enough.

That is one of the reasons why I wanted to write this book, so that it would motivate the parent. Never forget that the labor you put into with your children will affect them for the rest of their lives.

The key things that will help a student to achieve his permit are: the notes he takes in the classroom part of driver education and studying the handbook that he should have gotten from that class.

Most states provide a manual of some type that you can pick up at the local license examiner's office. You will need to help your son or daughter study for this by testing him or her on what he or she knows before he or she goes to take the test. As the parent, you should view the permit test as a serious exam that your child takes at school. The license examiners have busy days, and it has to be very frustrating for them to give test to someone more than once.

A lot of people think the test they take at the license examiners is made to trick people. That is not the case at all. The material on the test is not like the same material on most tests. It is there to make you think about your answer. Thinking is the key component used in driving safely. The test may word things confusingly. My advice is to know the hand book, or manual, and notes from driver education (if you have attended one in your state). You will not be wasting your time, because this is the stuff you will need for a lifetime of safe driving. The more you have in your head, the more available it will be in time of need.

I would like to close this book by sharing some of the years of experience I had with students in the classroom and behind the wheel. I have had students that would have difficulties getting out of a parking lot. Anyone that was watching would think the student was trying to drive a stick-shift car, or manual. Of course it was an automatic, but the swinging of our heads made it look otherwise.

It is really interesting how you have to be

careful with what you say to students. You may have a student that has been driving for a while, and you may say a phrase like, "Ready to get back on the road?" The next thing you know, the student may start trying to drive backwards all the way out of the parking lot.

Students will pull out onto the road and sometimes start to drive on the wrong side. As long as nothing is coming, I will let them momentarily do this, and then I will say something like, "We are not in England, you know."

Students will also freeze up on you in the worse possible spots. They will go to make a right turn and stop right in the middle of it. Young drivers will sometimes pull you head-on with other traffic or jerk the wheel when they run off the road or even when they think they're going to run off. I have also had students to try to make a left turn when traffic was coming.

God has really given me very good protection through the years with so many students. In ten years, I have only been in two wrecks. The first accident I was working with a student on listening to instructions. Like a lot of students I drive, he did not trust what I was telling him and he wanted to do his own thing.

We were getting ready to go out of a parking lot when I instructed the driver to go left. He did not want to turn and headed straight toward the curb and jammed on the brakes. I told the driver he could cause a rear-end collision and he should have listened to my instructions.

Only a few minutes later, as we were going down a road, a squirrel ran out in front of us, and I immediately said, "Do not slam on the brakes," and the driver did anyway. A van was tailgating and rammed into our rear.

The last wreck I was in, the student driver did not do anything wrong. A car ran a stop sign and ran into my door side. We were approaching a railroad crossing and going very slowly. I was instructing my driver about looking thoroughly for a train, and a car came out of a side street quickly into our car. If I had a gas pedal on my side, I may have had time to prevent this.

Although I have had two wrecks, that is not bad considering all the thousands of hours I have spent in a driver education car. All the safety procedures I have used over the years have really made a difference, and it can make a difference for you and your children if you are willing to learn them and put them into practice every time you drive.

When I teach classrooms, I do not just see a class full of students. What I see is a class full of people that need instruction on how to make it safely through their lives. I know there will be a massive amount of difficulties, trials, and tests brought before each and every student as they drive for the rest of their lives, but I want to make an impact on their lives, and I know it is important for parents to keep that process going.

Just as God requires children to obey their parents, parents need to love their children. Parents need to go through all the necessary means to teach them what is right. I urge all parents to not let these tender years of their children's lives slip through their fingers, but to communicate with their children, spend time with them, and to not give up on their children by just letting them go their own ways.

Let your instruction be good and let your relationship be even better. For most people, driving will be a lifelong learning process. To be safe drivers, we need habits that will stick with us for a long life of driving.

<u>About the Author</u>

Terry Lynn Moore is a licensed driver instructor with more than twelve thousand hours of experience with new drivers and over ten years experience in the classroom.

He is a member of the North Carolina Driver Traffic Safety Education Association.

Terry has a desire for teenagers, and all drivers, to be safer on the roads where millions of accidents and thousands of deaths occur each year.